Christmas
emotions

Christmas
emotions

Per Benjamin

Max van de Sluis

Tomas De Bruyne

life³
a bundle of creativity

stichting
kunstboek

Content

What is the beauty of Christmas?

TOMAS Christmas reminds us of some universal values which are often ignored in our hectic existence, such as the everlasting family ties, the giddy depths of love and the nourishing warmth of friendship. Aren't we fortunate that Christmas returns every year?

MAX Christmas is so many things! A time of looking back, a time of peace and quiet and most of all a time of gathering with family and friends. Everyone comes together preparing the food and flowers, getting in the mood for a warm, cosy, stress-free and social meal, having time for each other.

PER I agree with both of you, but for me personally the beauty lies in the time from the first days of Advent up until Christmas Eve. All the preparations, expectations, the whole excitement that is in the air: Christmas is on its way! All the small pre-Christmas gatherings, Christmas Eve and then some days just to relax, reflect and have time for doing nothing. It's a wonderful cycle!

7

What does Christmas mean to you?

MAX For me, as long as I can remember, the days before Christmas have been long, full of hard work and little sleep, if any. But at the same time it's one of the most enjoyable weeks of the whole year in the flower shop: a great working atmosphere, wonderful creations and that special smell of pine. That is when I really get into the Christmas spirit!

PER I can only agree! That warm friendly atmosphere with all the excitement in the air: that's what Christmas is all about for me. There might be lots of stress because time is as always short, but even in the last days of panic shopping there is time for a smile and some nice words. People seem more content than during other times of the year!

TOMAS Well, that's all very true, but I also try to see the inner values of the holiday: warmth, happiness and the joy among family and friends. It goes beyond the Christian celebrations, it's about getting together, enjoying each other's company and also about setting new goals for the future. After Christmas we start a new episode in our lives.

What is the most important message of Christmas?

TOMAS Like I just said, being together and understanding that we are all one and that by helping others we are also helping ourselves.

PER Exactly, that is so true. What we get out of Christmas as adults is the satisfaction of helping and making others happy! It is the best of times for sharing and giving.

MAX I know that it is easier said then done, but I really wish that all of us could live in harmony and peace and that we could all respect one another; that injustice was gone and that everyone had the same fine medical care, food and general quality of life. That is the true message of Christmas.

How do you celebrate Christmas yourselves?

TOMAS   I still like the traditional way of celebrating. I love the preparations and coming home to my parents with all my brothers and sisters. It is all still like when I was a child, sitting around the table, chatting, sharing emotions and enjoying each others' company!

MAX   Christmas Eve is spent with friends: an ever growing group of wives, husbands, boyfriends, lovers and children. It's an evening we all look forward to with anticipation. Christmas day is reserved for the family: a traditional celebration with all the right foods and drinks. This all makes Christmas the most beautiful time of the year!

PER   In December we have the tradition of 'Glöggfester', i.e. drinking mulled wine in friendly gatherings in a more causal but warm atmosphere with friends. Christmas Eve is all family business in the spirit of traditions. A day for coming together, eating too much of the wonderful food, having lots of good drinks, topped off with long discussions over party games.

Why are flowers so important at Christmas?

MAX   Flowers create that special Christmas atmosphere, today and as far back in history as we can see. Flowers are important troughout the year, but even more so at Christmas.

TOMAS   Yes, there is no Christmas without flowers and their scents! Flowers brighten up people's lives in this dark time of the year. From the welcoming wreath on the door to the flowers on the dinner table, they are all part of Christmas.

PER   Tradition is strong here in Sweden! I still have all the scents of Christmas from my childhood lingering in my mind. The gifts are not the only things I remember. The flowers simply bear so may positive memories, that we can not be without them.

That is interesting. Will people only want traditional compositions then?

PER   Absolutely not! We have the need for tradition when it comes to scents and some very essential materials. But we need to redefine and reinvent them, creating contemporary designs as well as traditional ones, perfectly executed.

What, then, is the future for Christmas flowers?

MAX I believe in a combination of traditional and contemporary designs; maybe use traditional flowers in modern ways or make a traditional arrangement or shape with new flowers or colours. It is important to hold on to the traditions, but at the same time you still have to follow the spirit of time!

PER Beautifully said! Interpreting the traditions, recreating and making them suitable for today's interiors and design is the most intriguing of challenges for today's flower designers. There are Christmas flowers for each and every interior, no matter what style, colour or expression!

Which are the most important materials that you associate with Christmas?

MAX For me they are mostly natural materials: pine (both needles and cones), berries of all kinds, Ilex, cranberries, beautiful moss-covered branches, nicely coloured twigs … all with an emotional, strong message.

TOMAS I fully agree with Max: adding the beauty of Larix branches, Poinsettias of all kinds and colours and more cones.

PER Being the less naturally inspired of us, I have to ditch most mosses and branches and use a heap of colourful materials and lots of flowers even such as the ordinary carnation and Chrysanthemum; all to play with concept and colours of Christmas creating a contemporary twist on traditional designs.

Talking about flowers: which ones do you prefer to use and why?

MAX I have a whole list of them, like e.g. Poinsettia (also known as Euphorbia pulcherrima), Ilex, mistletoe etc. They are all classical and for me they carry an emotional connection with Christmas. I like using them all, but mostly in a new and different way.

PER I think I am the one working with the widest variation of flowers for Christmas. I don't look as much to the individual feeling of the flower, but more to the expression of the finished composition. If that says Christmas, than each individual material is of minor importance

TOMAS I agree with Max here, tradition is the most important factor for me as well.

What is your favourite flower for Christmas?

TOMAS   I have several favourites, but I cherish all kinds of Helleborus flowers the most. The personality of these flowers expresses my feelings and my way of thinking perfectly.

MAX   I definitely agree! It is a pure, clean flower with a strong personality. One of the first flowers coming up in the midst of this dark period. Fragile and strong at the same time.

PER   The smell of white hyacinths: that is Christmas to me! Surprising I know, as most people see it as a real spring flower, but for us in Sweden it is the Christmas flower, even beating the Poinsettia!

What colours do you relate to Christmas?

PER   There are a whole lot of them, but without a doubt the most important for us in Sweden are of course all shades of warm reds and the winter crisp whites. Today, interestingly enough, we see a development of new colour spectra influenced by traditional materials like pine cones, straw and in smaller portions salmons and pinks. Times are definitely changing for the better!

TOMAS   The traditional colours will always be around. This red and green feeling will stay in all trends. But we should always remain open to new ideas and new combinations of colours to give each Christmas period its own atmosphere.

MAX   Yes, red and green will always be the most important. However, even more important is the emotional side of colours, they need to be connected with the people and the place where Christmas is celebrated.

How is Christmas changing in today's society?

TOMAS   What used to be a very traditional celebration is now changing into a very different event. Today we prefer to spend Christmas with the people closest to our hearts, rather than only the very close family.

MAX   Yes, society is changing … and the religious message related to Christmas with it. We see an interesting fusion between tradition and self-expression based on our Christian religion.

PER   Christmas is more of an international holiday, irrespective of our religion or faith. Sharing the typical values of Christmas – friendship and joyfulness – reflects in all the different ways of celebrating. Our personal situation, family and location on this planet blend beautifully with traditions.

How and where would your dream Christmas be spent?

PER   With my loved ones! I am very much open to doing it differently every now and then, on a tropical island or any foreign place. But once in a while I need the cold, frostbitten, white landscape from my Swedish childhood. I never grow too old for an honest snowball fight, skiing and then back in front of the fireplace with warm wine and my loved ones around.

MAX   Yes, I would also love a white Christmas with ice on the canals, ice-skating, nice family walks and building snowmen in the garden. I have all those great memories from my childhood and I really wish my newborn daughter to experience the same!

TOMAS   Being a romantic guy, I can only imagine a traditional atmosphere! Feel the cold outside and then into the warmth indoors with loved ones around the Christmas table.

What was your idea behind this Christmas book?

MAX   This book is all about inspiration and showing the different possibilities with Christmas designs and celebrations in various atmospheres. It wants to show new directions in design for the future as well as the present! The world of flowers is changing according to the rest of the world.

TOMAS   I want to share both my passion and ideas for this profession and the beauty of flowers for each occasion of Christmas. Creativity without limitations!

PER   The challenge was to show the future for flowers at Christmas, how to open up the eyes of people to contemporary design in such a traditional context as Christmas. To show that there are so many different ways of working with both traditional and unexpected flowers for Christmas, for both traditional and modern interiors. Having the mix of the three of us should give everyone a great deal of inspiration, I hope!

What is the emotional side of flowers at Christmas?

MAX   Through flowers we can express ourselves, create a relaxed atmosphere, bring people closer together and easily instigate conversation. There's nothing else that has this kind of magic!

PER   Max has really captured the essence of it! Flowers affect all of our senses and that — combined with our childhood memories of Christmas — is what is often called the spirit of Christmas.

TOMAS   Yes, flowers really show the beauty of family bonds and friendship in this time of sharing and loving.

What do you want for Christmas?

TOMAS   I know it is a cliché, but I will say it nevertheless! I don't feel the urge to receive something material. The experience of being together is more than enough, but harmony in the world would be great!

Yes, but ... anything material then?

TOMAS   Well if it has to be a real gift, then something nicely wrapped with care and love and one of those lovely little cards. That will touch my heart!

MAX   I just wish that all my family and friends may stay in good health, so that we can celebrate Christmas together again next year. Materialistically ... anything personal with an emotional value.

PER   What can I say, other than the fact that I agree with my colleagues and that I wish you all a very Merry Christmas!

Love is in the air when angels are inviting.
They are the link between dreams and reality and on special occasions they even make your sweetest dreams come true.
Feel the presence of angels in the room: they are watching over and caring for this close family.
Enjoy the pleasures of the food and of each other's company and bathe in this atmosphere of intimacy. Family as one unit and love as binding factor.

invited
by angels

It starts with a welcoming glass of champagne. Take off your coat and feel at home. Pass through the cold grey entrance into a warmer grey-reddish room where the Christmas tree is decorated in a modern and inviting way. Leave your presents under the tree to unwrap them later at dinner.

Fill the room with
laughter and enjoy
a drink together.
Take the time to
enjoy your Christmas
dinner at a beautifully
decorated table.

Every member of the family is feeling the bond with their close ones. In this case grandfather and grandmother are inviting their four-generation family. They have opened both their house and their hearts for their beloved family members. Their home is a warm base for all and coming together at Christmas is a family event and a reason to appreciate the beauty of family every year.

Welcoming loved ones, family and distant friends!

Let feelings of love melt the walls of your troubled heart. (Tomas)

Joyful and full of expectations,
as we all are at Christmas time. (Per)

Christmas overkill,
more is definitely more! (Per)

36

It all circles around Christmas! (Per)

Traditional

For generations families have come together to celebrate Christmas. Over the years the Christmas atmosphere has become more and more important: preparations (both for food and decorations) start weeks before. For decades people have used the typical materials they could find outdoors like e.g. pine, pine cones, ilex, berries etc. They try to find the most spectacular tree, their outdoor decoration has to be the most beautiful of the street ... they spend a lot of time to make their homes as beautiful as they can. People often do these preparations together, because this time spent together is also a part of the real Christmas experience they don't want to miss out on.

The whole house is immersed in the Christmas atmosphere: from the front door through the hallway to the kitchen.

The smell of Christmas lingers through the house: the scent of those typically used materials combined with the mouthwatering aromas of the traditional food.

48

To top off this true Christmas emotion, the living room is filled with the sound of Christmas carols.
Then it's finally time to celebrate: the family enters the richly decorated house and gets in the perfect Christmas mood, reminiscing of all the years they've been celebrating this day together. Finally it's time for the children to open their presents under the tree: parents and grand-parents are proudly watching them, while thinking back to their own childhood.

After the little children have been put to bed, the finishing touches for the food are made in the richly decorated kitchen, to be subsequently served on the sumptuously decorated table. Everyone enjoys the traditional food and the company of each other, realizing that these are the important things in life.

51

Later the heart-warming conversations
will be continued on the couch,
accompanied by some good drinks.
These are the moments we will
remember for the rest of our lives.

Circle of warmth and hope! Tradition meets contemporary.

Bound X-mass (Max)

Pine cones! Nature's elegant simplicity,
transformed by the Christmas spirit! (Per)

Allow passion to bubble up to the surface
and colour your daily life. (Tomas)

63

Know yourself: true beauty comes from within. (Tomas)

Pure needles Unexpected Christmas feeling (Max)

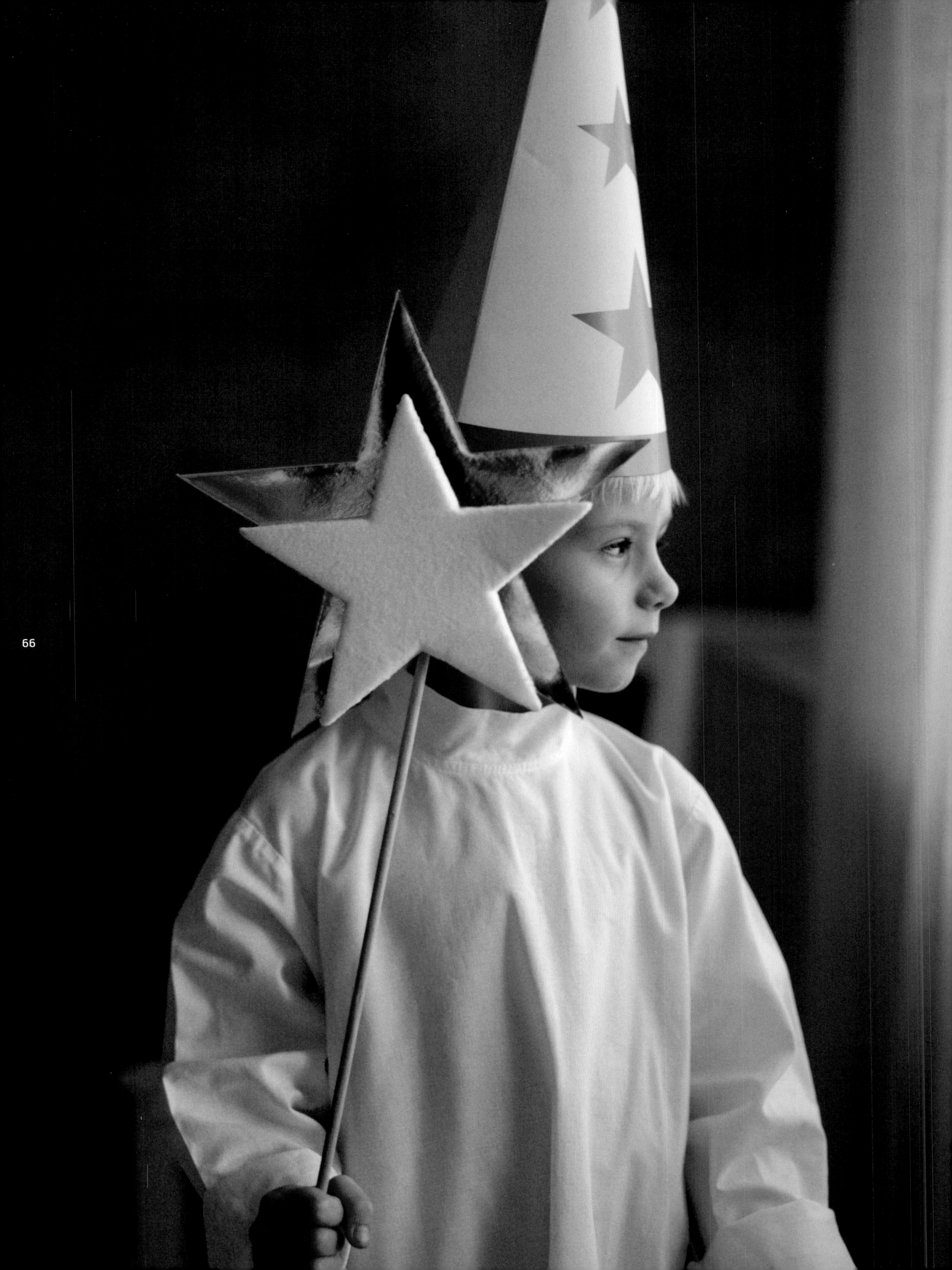

*Nightly, go heavy hearts
Round farm and steading
On earth, where sun departs,
shadows are spreading.
Then on our darkest night,
Comes with her shining light
Sankta Lucia! Sankta Lucia!*

*Then on our darkest night,
Comes with her shining light
Sankta Lucia, Sankta Lucia.*

Thus starts one of Sweden's most traditional Christmas/ Lucia songs. Lucia, originally an Italian saint, has been celebrated in its current tradition in Sweden since the early 1700s. On the morning of 13 December, the darkest day of the year, Lucia – a lady dressed in white with a candle-wreath in her hair – can be seen walking in procession in this celebration of light together with maidens and star boys, singing Christmas songs. In more familiar surroundings she comes serving morning coffee, our special saffron buns, *Lussebullar*, and cinnamon cookies, *Pepparkakor*, while singing this special Lucia song.

White story

Night-darkling, huge and still.
Hark! something's stirring!
In all our silent rooms,
Wingbeats are whisp'ring!
Stands on our threshold there,
White clad, lights in her hair,
Sankta Lucia! Sankta Lucia!

Stands on our threshold there,
White clad, lights in her hair,
Sankta Lucia! Sankta Lucia!

Today, every town in Sweden chooses its very own 'Lucia' for the year and celebrations take place in churches, workplaces, schools, homes and are shown on morning television.

Darkness shall fly away
Through earthly portals!
She brings such wonderful
words to us mortals!
Daylight, again renewed,
will rise, all rosy-hued!
Sankta Lucia! Sankta Lucia!

Daylight, again renewed,
will rise, all rosy-hued!
Sankta Lucia! Sankta Lucia!

A light in the long dark winter, a time of hope and rejoicing. (Per)

80

White X-mass (Max)

82

Pure (Max)

Modesty is the way to shine among pearls. (Tomas)

88

Fragility in motion (Tomas)

90

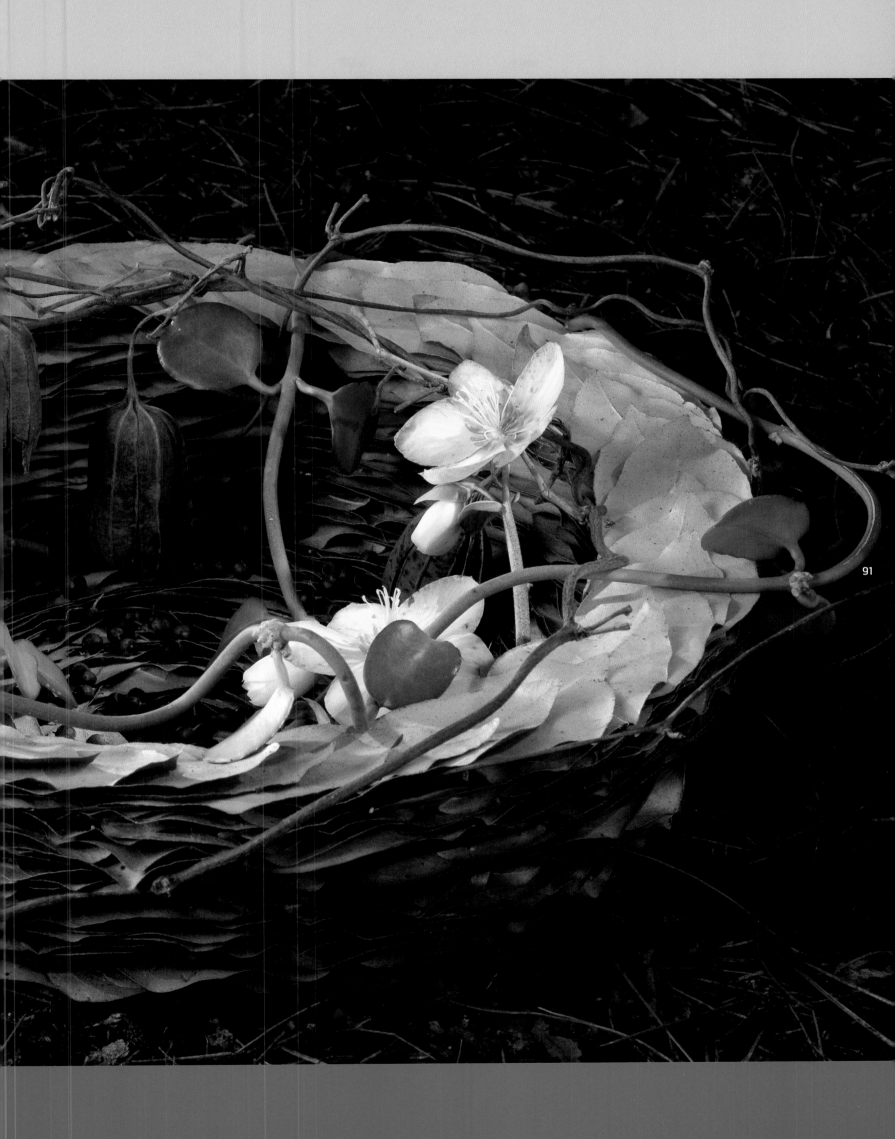

The old tradition of Christmas celebrations has gradually changed over the years and from generation to generation. Nowadays groups of friends celebrate it together. What once started as gatherings where college friends were having some drinks together, have now become more fancy and luxurious parties for these young professionals. They have become prestigious and competitive do's: every year the party has to be bigger, better and more stylish than last year's. The parties have become a sign of how good these people are doing in life. Every year someone else will organize the party, while the expenses are shared. These are the kind of parties that start late in the afternoon and go on until the early hours. Over the years these parties have become a tradition on their own.

New tradition

94

They meet each other in the lobby, which is decorated in a young and fanciful manner (since they want to be perceived as young and stylish): here they have some drinks together and talk about everything that is going on in their life.

Afterwards it's time for dinner: on colourful, nice, modernly decorated tables they have their long dinner together.

They will have a lot of drinks, but won't need to worry because everybody will stay in the hotel. Since the college days are over, they live all over the country. Tonight nobody wants to go home and miss the end of the party.

It's time for relaxation in the playfully decorated lounge bar. That's where the old strong stories from days gone by are told, that's where they will stay till late at night.

I did it my way. (Max)

Simply the colours of the cones! (Per)

Pine needles woven into magic! (Per)

Hanging – light – pure – X-mass (Max)

Red is the colour and apple the thing! Christmas, is it not? (Per)

112

Shelter the ones you love so they can grow in perfect harmony. (Tomas)

Black story

Modern people want to maintain the traditions, but in new and expressive ways! Traditions need to be adjusted and modernised in order to meet the demands of 21st century life.

We are celebrating Christmas in new atmospheres and many times with new constellations of people, new kinds of families and friends ,all mixed together.

The essence of Christmas
is changing from materialistic
into something

122

But please, do not leave the typical Christmas flowers behind! Reinvent them, give them a new look that matches you and your home. Remember that flowers can communicate who you are and what you want! The Christmas star is still there, but in black. The flowers are the same traditional ones, Hippeastrum and Ilex, in the colour red, but in new combinations, mixed with exotic flowers. All in a wide range of reds together with the always cool and trendy black.

124

The new black! Everything and everyone looks good in black. It is a warm, inviting and honest colour if that is what you want it to be! Merry Christmas!

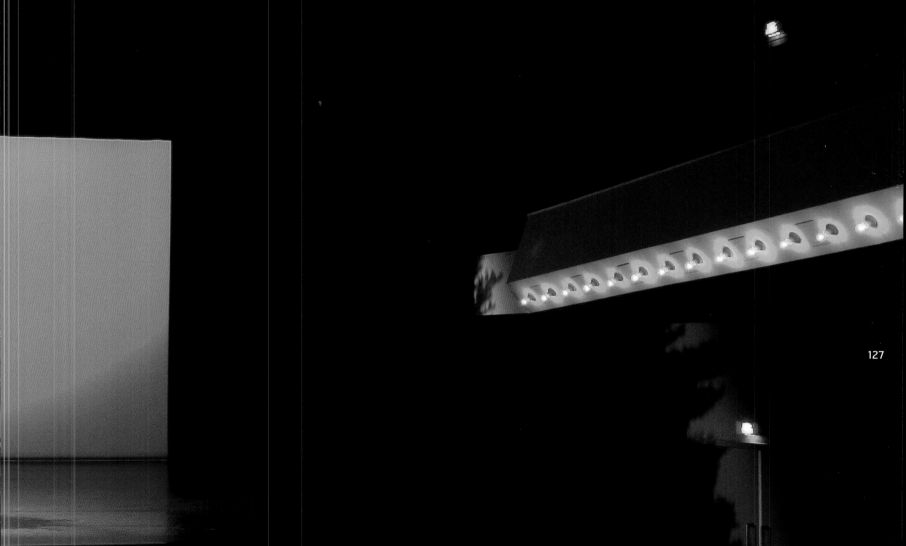

Let subtle elegance wrap itself around the flow of your life. (Tomas)

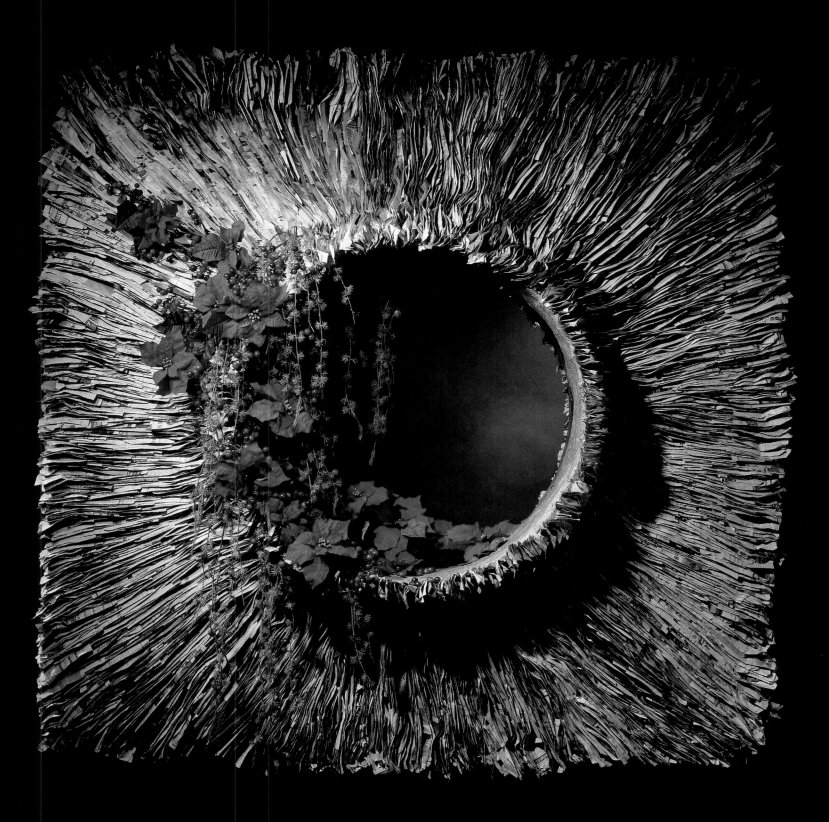

A touch of Christmas (Tomas)

133

Draw from life's experiences and rise stronger then before,
like a phoenix from the ashes. (Tomas)

Where there's a will, there's a way. (Tomas)

Complex simplicity (Max)

Draw strength from the purity of your heart. (Tomas)

140

Rough purity (Max)

A Christmas party

No better occasion to meet up with your friends than for sharing Christmas together.

Pay special attention to the entrance hall, so people will experience a warm and unique welcome to your home.

Invite them to the glass table,
decorated with candles and food.

148

Let them taste the buffet and surprise them with a *smörgåsbord* of tastes. Enjoy a relaxed atmosphere among friends without any rules or obligations.

Give the party a special theme like in this case: the twenties and thirties. Let this period inspire you when choosing your outfit and look forward to enjoying an unforgettable evening together with your best friends.
Allow your friends to get to know each other while chatting away in a cosy room, lit by candles and decorated with special Christmas attributes.

14

Invited by angels 15

Rosa
Larix

 16

 17

Moss musgo
Larix
Different berries

18 19

Moss musgo
Helleborus
Pinus strobus
Cineraria maritima
Phalaenopsis
Larix

 26 27

 28 29

30 31

Phalaenopsis
Larix
Jasminum

Fructus Rosa
Fructus Eucalyptus
Fructus Alnus

Cristal
Coal
Phalaenopsis

152

 38 39

 40  41

42 43

Tradition

Cornus alba 'Sibirica'
Sarracenia
Oxycoccus macrocarpus

Dianthus
Celosia
Rosa
Limonium 'Emille'
Cymbidium

Phalaenopsis
Oncidium
Fructus Eucalyptus

Ilex aquifolium 'Argentea Marginata'
Ilex verticillata
Fructus Malus
Skimmia japonica 'Rubella'
Capsicum

 50 51

 52 53

 54 55

Cyclamen
Anthurium andreanum
Phalaenopsis
Vuylstekeara cambria 'Plush'
Moss
Rubus fruticosus
Araucaria
Euphorbia pulcherrima
Oxycoccus macrocarpus

Oxycoccus macrocarpus
Epidendrum
Cyclamen
Phalaenopsis

Fructus Malus
Ilex verticillata
Gloriosa rothschildiana

20 21 22 23 24 25

Rosa
Different berries

Pinus strobus
Rosa
Different berries
Larix

Pinus strobus
Rosa
Different berries
Larix

32 33 34 35 36 37

Hippeastrum
Nerine
Hypericum
Panicum
Celosia
Xanthorrhoea australis

Phalaenopsis
Cyclamen
Epidendrum
Ludisia
Anthurium andreanum

Malus
Passiflora
Oxycoccus macrocarpus

Hippeastrum
Ilex verticillata
Fructus Malus

153

44 45 46 47 48 49

Malus
Cornus alba 'Sibirica'
Oxycoccus macrocarpus
Aranda 'Pannee'

Abies nordmanniana
Oxycoccus macrocarpus
Hippeastrum
Hyacinthus

Abies nordmanniana
Cornus alba 'Sibirica'
Betula
Ilex aquifolium 'Argentea
Marginata'
Ilex verticillata

Strelitzia reginae
Fructus Malus
Oxycoccus macrocarpus

56 57 58 59 60 61

Cornus alba 'Sibirica'
Euphorbia pulcherrima
Phalaenopsis
Pinus
Cattleya
Cyclamen
Hedera helix 'Arborescens'
Fructus Malus
Passiflora

Fructus Pinus
Ilex verticillata
Cymbidium
Fructus Malus
Anthurium 'Choco'

Betula branches
Red berries

Cotton balls
Larix
Helleborus niger
Cineraria

Pinus
Paphiopedilum
Phalaenopsis
Ceropegia sandersonii
Kalanchoe
Cryptomeria japonica

Hippeastrum
Picea
Tillandsia xerographica
Gypsophila
Euphorbia pulcherrima
Eucharis

Gypsophila
Tillandsia xerographica
Picea
Eucharis
Calocephalus brownii

Triticum aestivum
Ilex verticillata
Guzmania

154

Saintpaulia
Cineraria maritima

Helleborus niger

Elaeagnus
Aristologia
Helleborus niger
Ceropegia sandersonii

Phalaenopsis
Epidendrum
Ceropegia sandersonii
Vanda

Vanda
Abies koreana

Paphiopedilum leeanum
Phalaenopsis
Euphorbia pulcherrima
Anthurium andreanum
Viscum album
Hedera helix 'Arborescens'

68  **69**

70  **71**

72  **73**

Tillandsia xerographica
Calocephalus brownii
Gypsophila

Dianthus
Eucharis
Tillandsia xerographica
Nerine
Picea
Calocephalus brownii

Dianthus
Eucharis
Tillandsia xerographica
Nerine
Picea
Calocephalus brownii

80  **81** **82**  **83**

84  **85**

Mitsumata
Helleborus niger
Cyclamen
Passiflora

Phalaenopsis
Tillandsia xerographica

Chrysanthemum
Rosa
Nerine
Euphorbia pulcherrima
Ilex verticillata

Fructus Eucalyptus
Tricitum aestivum

155

92  **93** **94**  **95** **96**  **97**

Cornus alba 'Sibirica'
Tulipa 'Rococo'
Philodendron 'Imperial Red'
Schefflera

Epidendrum
Aristologia
Vanda
Abies koreana
Oncidium

Oncidium roots
Elaeagnus
Pinus

Vanda
Phalaenopsis
Anthurium andreanum
Hedera helix 'Arborescens'
Arachnus

Gerbera
Ilex verticillata
Ceropegia sandersonii

104  **105** **106**  **107** **108**  **109**

Fructus Picea
Dianthus
Chrysanthemum
Rosa
Hypericum
Limonium 'Emille'
Panicum
Celosia
Magnolia

Pinus japonica
Euphorbia pulcherrima
Skimmia japonica
Gerbera germini
Rosa 'Passion'
Ilex verticillata
Fructus Malus

Phalaenopsis
Helleborus niger
Kalanchoe blossfeldiana
Ludisia

Gloriosa rothschildiana
Nerine bowdenii
Vanda
Fructus Malus

Pinus strobus
Helleborus niger

Guzmania
Vriesea
Ilex verticillata
Hippeastrum
Nerine bowdenii
Picea

Ligustrum
Paphiopedilum

Hippeastrum
Ligustrum
Xanthorrhoea australis

Hippeastrum
Ligustrum
Paphiopedilum
Ilex verticillata
Nerine bowdenii
Picea

Xerophyllum
asphodeloides

Abies koreana
Ceropegia sandersonii
Epidendrum
Ludisia
Arachnus

Helleborus niger
Coal

Mitsumata
Pinus
Rhododendron simsii

Eucharis grandiflora
Cineraria

Helleborus
Ranunculus
Kalanchoe 'Calandiva'

Helleborus
Ranunculus
Kalanchoe 'Calandiva'

Helleborus

Paphiopedilum
Ligustrum
Cymbidium
Zantedeschia
Fructus Malus
Ilex verticillata

Cymbidium
Ligustrum
Fructus Malus
Rosa 'Black Baccara'
Dianthus

Guzmania
Nerine bowdenii

Euphorbia pulcherrima
Ligustrum

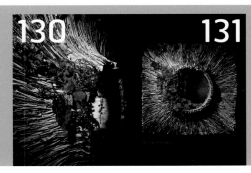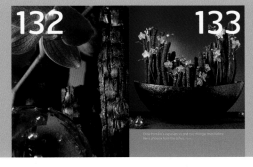

Spathiphyllum
Black pepper

Poinsettia
Larix
Rosehip

Branches
Phalaenopsis

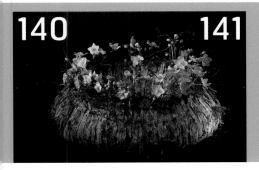

Helleborus niger
Betula
Pinus

Malus
Buxus sempervirens

Buxus sempervirens

158

From Per:

My family: for being there for me, for all your encouragement and support. You are the best supporters anyone can wish for!

Classe: the one who gets all the behind the scene stuff! You suffer when I do, are ecstatically happy when I am, try to hang on and understand the process of creativity! But most of all I want to thank you for supporting and encouraging me. Love you!

My friends: for reminding me there is more in life than flowers. Because there are other things ... even though these flowers are quite nice!

Johan: for always helping me into the late hours, a true assistant!

Nicklas: Long time friend and college, it's always a lot of fun working together with you! Remember though: you can do two things at a time! ;-)

Jonathan: For being the true Englishman you are and for putting the right words where they should be.

Helén and Zelda: my photographer and her little daughter. What can I say: you are not only a sharp photographer but also one great woman/mother, handling both Zelda and the camera at the same time!

Hukra: once again you let me haunt you with my difficult requests! Thanks for your sponsorship, for your support and for sharing my view on flower design.

Rasmus and Wilma: you were just great! Who could have known you where small 'catwalk' wannabes! Could not have gotten a better 'Star-boy' and Lucia maid. And yes: we will keep those trains a secret ;-)

Sara: the Lucia in the worldwide scene of flowers from now on! You are the carrier of Swedish tradition and beauty. Hope your husband and kids enjoyed it!

Jonas: this is what I call routine! Already looking forward to your performance in the next coming title ... ;-)

Mattias: for turning your diary upside down. Cool and with that toothpaste commercial smile of yours! You were perfect!

Linda: Express beauty! One could think that you do nothing else all day than looking cool and mingling at parties.

Everyone else that helped along the way: for giving a hand or a comforting word. You are not forgotten.

From Max:

Kathy: for all your support and patience and especially for Rachel.

Jan and Mieke, my friends: for opening up your house for my flowers and for all your help. It was a very special day we will never forget.

My mother and father: for your never-ending patience and all the work you do for me.

Ester: for being my right hand and for working through all those long nights: I don't know how I would do it without you.

Hanky, Loes, Bjorn and Tino: for all your hard work, the good times and the humour. You reminded us of why we do this job. Thanks!

Jeroen: thanks for everything, for searching for the locations for your students of the Citaverde college (www.citaverde.nl) and overall for your enthusiasm and helping hands.

Deluxe Hotel Derlon: for opening your doors for the photography, this was fabulous. Thanks. (www.derlon.nl)

Pim: We did it again, the long days but with a lot of fun and humour. Thanks.

Theatre 't Voorhuys Emmeloord: Rob, thanks for the lighting and for your time.

Everyone else who helped me with this and with other projects, you are not forgotten.

From Tomas:

My friends, whom I want to dedicate this book to. Their support and their mere existence have made this book possible. They have showed me that beauty and pureness also exist beside flowers.

Kristel, thank you for introducing me to the wonderful world of flowers. You were my first teacher and you will always have a special place in my heart.

Jinny, my special friend. For your dedication and support to me as a person and flower designer.

Hanky, what would I have done without you during the process of making this book? You pushed and helped me from the start till the end. And to discover you had hidden talents as a photo stylist ;-)

My mother and my sister Hilde, for your relentless support, your wisdom and unconditional love.

My florist colleagues who helped making the arrangements. I had the feeling they put all their heart into it and mustered a special energy. What can I say: a wonderful team: Hanky, Petra, Leonidas, Asselien and Alex.

The photographers. Kurt, you did it again! You are capable of freezing a moment of beauty by using your lens. My friends, Michelle and Xavier, your dedication was great.

The people and companies who facilitated me with their services and products and made everything more beautiful: Micheline Biot, Agora, Serax, Van Remoortel, O-Living, Het Wilgenbroek, Slots NV, Flamant Interiors, Annetics, Geert De Puysseleyr, Herman Borglevens.

The location was superb, thanks to both families for opening their homes to me and my team: Huis Van Wonterghem and Mrs Van Der Eecken. Without you and the intimacy of your homes, it could never have been the same atmosphere.

The models, this time too many to mention, but briefly: Family Berquin, Jill and Helen

Thanks to everybody for creating and sharing moments and occasions for our souls to grow.

Authors:
Per Benjamin (SE)
Max van de Sluis (NL)
Tomas De Bruyne (BE)

Photographers:
Kurt De Keyzer (BE)
Michelle Francken (BE)
Helén Pe (SE)
Pim van der Maden (NL)
Jeong Gyu-Hyeon (KOR): p. 131-132

Final editing:
Femke De Lameillieure

Layout & Colour separations:
Group Van Damme, Oostkamp (BE)

Printed by:
Group Van Damme, Oostkamp (BE)

Published by:
Stichting Kunstboek bvba
Legeweg 165
B-8020 Oostkamp
Tel.: + 32 50 46 19 10
Fax: + 32 50 46 19 18
E-mail: info@stichtingkunstboek.com
www.stichtingkunstboek.com

ISBN: 978-90-5856-240-1
D/2007/6407/14
NUR: 421